Momma Maralyn,
You are truly so precious. I have truly enjoyed your presence and your smile.
Love,
Myla De

Dawn: Diary of a Poet

by Myla Denise

Foreword by
Thomas G. Wright

Published and Distributed by:
Cole Publishing Company
13428 Maxella Avenue #701
Marina Del Rey, CA 90292
310-330-9937

Cover Design by
Paula White
Paula White Designs

First Printing: April 2005
ISBN 0-9778779-9-7

Formatting & Editing Team:
Myla Denise
Donna McDuffie

The set up of the book is great. Every thought and every line flows together. It's beautiful. Readers can tell that everything is genuine and comes straight from the heart. Each section allows the reader to know where Denise was, where she went, where she was going, and where she ended up; complete, totally healed and equipped to help others be free. I was able to follow [the author's] journey through Dawn and see that the way to win was not to hurt anybody, but to open yourself up, have hope, obtain healing and be set free. [Then] you can help others struggling with a similar situation and be who God called you to be so you can be in His perfect will and plan for your life.

Regardless of what a person is going through even if the experience is not the same, after reading Dawn there's no way, they can walk away without a word or a phrase that touches them to the point where they are encouraged enough to keep on going and not be defined by their situation or circumstance but by who God said they were and would be. This book really touched me.

-Chanda Long
Singer/Songwriter
Founder and Owner, Ex-C.E.L. Entertainment, Detroit, MI

You have no idea what you have in your hand! This is a must read for any individual who seeks to truly live and master life on the next level. This is the mandatory corridor that one must take if you are to arrive at your destiny. This great work courageously magnetizes you page by page to journey into the inner you. The prize in journeying there is to know that when you get there, God is there. Healing happens inside out and not outside in. What a mastery of language and poetical expression. Outstanding! [Denise is] now the lyrical/poetical Moses for many. God Bless!

-Rev. Richard E. Wilford
Pastor
New Bethel Missionary Baptist Church, Gary, IN

Dawn is a life altering experience. It is the voice of millions as spoken by one Myla Denise, whose exceptional gift of expression takes each reader on a journey of self-discovery, forgiveness and healing. Dawn is a passage filled with pain and joy; hurt and healing. May the message of hope and restoration as it is written in Dawn take you from your valley into the presence of God where healing is and destiny begins.

-Elder Keyonda S. McQuarters
Co-Founder, KM Ministries
Radio host, Keys to Living, Chicago, IL

Dedication

This collection of poetry is dedicated to you who have used what should have set you up for failure lead you into greatness. You know who you are and you should be proud. I know I am.

Acknowledgments

I'm grateful to my parents, Regina McCloud and Mark Edmond I, for giving me life and for loving me. Please know that I feel and trust your love for me. Evangeline and Joseph McCloud; Lillian and James Edmond, I couldn't have asked for better grandparents. I know how fortunate I am to have the four of you in my life. I love you all very much and I am proud to be called your granddaughter. Mark II and Madison, thank you for making me want to be better so that I could be a better example for you.

Because this book was so difficult for me to even consider publishing, it took the prayers, support and encouragement from a strong circle of people that I am proud and honored to call my friends. You all have gently pushed me through every phase and I am truly grateful to you for that. The last few years have been emotionally exhausting and each one of you have served as a piece of my foundation. You have helped hold me together when I thought it'd be easier to just give up and fall apart. I will always hold a special place in my heart for you.

Jelecia Hoskins, I have appreciated and loved your excitement over my words. You gave me the confidence early on to pursue what I was too afraid to. Thank you for believing in me and dreaming big with me.

Lena Quintero, you took it upon yourself to live through these poems with me and I love you so much for that. Thank you for the many expressions of you love you send, especially the infamous Soooooul Care Bible. Preach!

Chanda Long, you were the first person to tell me that I needed to write this story. At the time, I was not trying to hear you, but I realize that you planted that seed way back then. So this really is all your fault (smile) and I sincerely thank you.

Pastor Wilford, thank you for being a part of this process. Your thoughts concerning this project were encouraging and your words reminded me of the reason why I had to proceed.

Thomas Wright, thank you for speaking such powerful words of encouragement into my life. You always had a way of making me believe I could do anything. I definitely appreciate it and I'm concerned because nothing's wrong (smile).

Keyonda McQuarters, when we met I had no idea where we'd be going, but I'm so glad that we are on this journey together. Thank you for spiritually stretching me, especially when I didn't want any part of it. You have consistently told me the truth and tried to get me to recognize the strength I had within. And when everybody else was trying to rescue me, I thank you for just being what I really needed; a friend.

Candace Cole Kelly, before I met you, I knew that your presence in my life would alter it tremendously. Both professionally and personally you've set a strong, positive and godly example to me. I'm thankful to you for staying on me about this project and for showing me that I was always more important to you than the work. You took the time to check on me through various stages of this process and I love you for it. Feel free to sing your life's songs, I won't charge you for it (smile).

Autumn Jones, Michael Muse, Kendrah Sharpley and Rana Wright, you are my light and inspiration. I'm strong because I feed off of your strength.

Jan Benson, Shantell Johnson, Kila Jones, LaToya Jones, Michelle McGregor, Michelle McGuire, Sarah Mills and Monique Pointer, even if you don't realize it you played an important role in my being able to share this story now because you allowed me to share it with you then.

I don't want those who read my story to give me the credit for anything. My strength has come from my faith. My faith has been what has sustained me. The greatest thing I can ever say that I've done was be obedient. God has given me the strength to persevere. God has given me the will to proceed. God has given me the vision to show me that I have a future. God has given me the direction that has led me to pursue my life's work. All that I am and all that I have has been God given.

Foreword

Healing. Whether physical or spiritual, everyone has to go through some type of healing during their lifetime. It is inevitable. It is an integral part of the life cycle. Wounds occur. They can be simple or complicated. They can be deep and festering or barely scratching the surface. And through the natural course of time or by provocation, they should all come to a place of healing. A simple statement yes, but not always a simple process. One must account for that one ever-present tangible; pain.

Pain is a very determining factor in the longevity of the wound. Pain can cause the healing to be sought after with all due diligence or it can cause one to hide the wound, thus removing the source of the pain, even if it is fleeting. Pain, along with the location of the wound is the combination which determines the healing. If I injure my flesh, the pain can be immediate and relief is quickly found in whatever form to ease the pain, and bring about healing. If my spirit is injured, however the wound is not always prevalent and thus, healing is not always understood as a remedy. It all depends on the pain.

Dawn, in its eclectic collection of marvelously written prose, is an eye into the process of the life cycle of healing. Every thought provoking stanza walks you through from beginning to end. It is the some total of a journey into the life of one so bold, and yet so vulnerable. It is the story of an injury that occurred to the spirit by way of a violation of the flesh. And though the physical wounds were unseen, at least by those in close proximity, the spiritual wounds were deep and festering. If you say the natural course of action is to attack the wound to ease the pain and bring about the necessary healing, I would counter, "have you experienced such a wound that resulted in this type of pain?" Perhaps not this particular wound but one just as intense or painful.

Why is Dawn an important piece? I'm glad you asked. There is a line in one of the poems that I believe is the essence of this word. "And to be a true example the only way I can understand is to have gone where they are and stood where they stand." Dawn is not a whimsical compilation of a talented writer. The author is talented without question. It is a revelation to those who are still in pain from wounds old and new, deep and festering that have buried the process and thereby, hindered their own healing. Dawn is a revelation to those trapped in a cell, unable to escape because they see and don't comprehend, listen but can't hear. I thank Denise with all my heart for having the courage to not sit on her gift, but offer direction to many, albeit, any who read this book.

Dawn is a way of escape. Do you dare?

-Thomas G. Wright
Instructor, Calvary Bible Institute
Greater Mount Calvary Holy Church, Washington, DC

Dawn: to become clear suddenly;
the initial stage in the process of development

There was a time when I adamantly did not want to do this. It's amazing how something like fear can keep people from their destiny. Poetry began as a way for me to express what I felt, but would not dare expose to anyone. When I started writing about a broader range of subjects, I would share, but only the ones I deemed nice. After a little coaxing and a lot of encouraging I realized that my poetry had the potential to help people in the same way that I was comforted when writing it. This is not to say that I didn't have any apprehension about publishing my most personal feelings, but what superceded my fear was the responsibility that began to tug on my heart. It dawned on me how selfish it would be to refuse to help others by hoarding a gift that God has given me in the first place.

No one's childhood is perfect and mine is no exception, but what I've discovered is that those of us with humble and troubled beginnings don't all end up with matching endings. We don't all turn to suicide or lives of promiscuity, drugs, alcohol and failure. Many of us stand up. Many of us lift our heads. Many of us live productive lives, maintain healthy relationships and continue. It's not that we don't struggle and don't have hurt-filled days, times when we're flooded with horrible memories, but we make a continuous daily effort and daily decision that today is not the day we'll be beaten.

This is to all my sisters and brothers who grew tired of being flat on their faces. Annoyed with crying, sick of taking it, refused to be professional victims, determined to stay in their right minds, willing to persevere and yet are still meek and have no need to broadcast their strength. What was intended to diminish your spirit has only deepened your soul. What was made to destroy your happiness has only elevated your joy. What was supposed to make you a failure has shown you just how much you are capable of. What was designed to make you ungrateful has made you so gracious. What could have made it difficult for you to open up has only made you more sincere. What should have made you impossible to love has only increased your capacity to care. What was intended to kill you has only made you rise up and fight. I recognize your power. I respect your choice. I am in awe of your courage.

As I step out on faith and share my spiritual dawn with you, I hope that it becomes clear to you that if God can do this for me, and this is all his doing, he can do the same for you. This book solely exists because he does. If you haven't quite reached your dawn, I pray that something written in the pages that follow will help you get there, for joy truly does come in the morning!

...I urge you to live a life worthy of the calling you have received.
Ephesians 4:1

Author's Note

This book consists of a collection of poetry, as well as actual entries from journals that I keep. The poems along with the journal entries paint a very real and honest picture of life, in all its heartbreak and hope. By the end of this uniquely told story, my prayer is that you will recognize that even when pain is at its peak, it still can't eclipse the smallest glimmer of hope.

I recognize that the subject matter of this material may be difficult for some to read, especially those in my family, but please know that it is not my intent to hurt anyone. I had to follow my heart and this project, as difficult and painful as it was, is part of my life's work. I hope you can look past the pain to see the glory. I thank every member of my family, in advance, for not allowing this project to destroy the joy we have when we're together because of the love we have for one another.

Myla Denise

Table of Contents

Valley Days

Dawn: Diary of a Poet

Another Fight

Tossing and turning all last night
can't believe there was another fight
punches were thrown, I got kicked around
but I wouldn't fight back, simply kept my head down
not to take cover, that wouldn't have helped
basically I sat and took it, didn't even yell
the wounds sting, the pain is intense
I can't understand why I put myself through this
the battle was fierce, but there were no marks
the places I got hit left invisible scars
I beat up on myself with my negative sentiments
and each time I feel like such a hypocrite
for not living in the knowledge I've been given
or living the life that I know I should be living
that the person I should be most dependent on for love and respect
hasn't fully grasped that concept in her heart yet
a constant battle between what I know and what my heart believes
allowing the knowledge in my head to deceive me
assuming that because I know what I'm supposed to do
that my heart will one day follow suit
but if that was true I wouldn't be nursing my wounds tonight
I've beat up on myself on yet another fight
mad at myself for not being all I think I should be
and for seeing the things about myself that I see
hard on myself for not reaching the goals I've set
upset for not wiping memories out of my mind yet
wondering why I expect so much out of myself
things I'd never require out of anyone else
telling myself I need to talk to someone who cares
but then disappointed for even needing to share
on opposite ends of the same emotional spectrum
unsure where this unrealistic expectation comes from
waiting for me to be more tolerant and patient with myself
and for love to come from within instead of someone else

captivity

so many thoughts
voiceless feelings
memories of yesterday
old beginnings
wanting to be cured
so I can move on
but I am for sure
that this has just begun
admission is the start
countless times I've spoken the words
but only on the outside
my heart hasn't heard
telling the story
without emotion
in order to avoid
an internal commotion
feelings are concealed
not allowed to reach
the surface of my soul
becoming a security breach
I can't let myself feel
my heart couldn't take it
if I open up to this
I'm not sure I'd make it
my so-called solution
smile the pain away
even if it's fake
I'm smiling in faith
only getting an extension
on what is bound to occur
a breakthrough accompanied by
a great deal of hurt
how can my heart handle
what my mind isn't able
to get a full grasp on
and still remain stable
and how can I expect
to get past this point
if the healing process
is what I desperately avoid
it will not just go away
no matter how much I try

Dawn: Diary of a Poet

to act like it doesn't affect me
and internalize that lie
everyday is a struggle
me trying to maintain
that my worth is not dependent
on the source of my pain
that I am not a reflection
of what I had to persevere
that I'm not the same little girl
who walked around in fear
that my past may be a part of me
but it does not define
who I am and what I'll be
in my lifetime
one day I will let myself
completely be released
so that this negativity
can stop having a hold on me
but before it can release it's hold
I have to set it free
I've kept it bound inside my heart
no wonder I'm in captivity

Diary Entries

I don't know what is going on with me, but I don't feel particularly close to anyone. I feel emotionally shut off. Like someone shut off my capacity to feel.

*****

I'm truly considering going to see a therapist. Last night I broke down on the phone while talking to [a friend]. I'm not sure what triggered these thoughts, but my stomach has been queasy off and on since last night. She picked me up and I stayed the night at her apartment. I felt like I was actually going through one incident all over again. I really experienced a physical pain in my body last night. I am kind of scared because I truly thought that I could handle this but it's gotten the best of me once again. I've got so much emotion backed up in my heart that it's ridiculous. I really wish they had never ever touched me. It's causing entirely too much drama for me. I was told to just stop thinking about it. I wish it was that simple.

*****

I wrote a poem that I can't stop reading. It's called Constantly Fighting. It's so honest. It shows that it is a constant fight. It doesn't just go away. Even after spending time in God's presence there are still moments. Still times when I have to fight to hold on to peace of mind. I want to tell people that so they won't feel bad for having to face those memories again and again. The thing is, just continue fighting. Continue pushing. Continue praying. It does pay off.

Dawn: Diary of a Poet

Constantly Fighting

constantly fighting off the hands that have touched my mind
as they found their way around my neck, between my legs and up my spine
taking me to hurtful places as his face tells of his pleasure
breaking me into a million fragments left to piece myself back together
remnants of his decision hinders my ability to be intimate
causing his face to show up at times when others try to be affectionate
I know he doesn't belong there, but I don't know to make him leave
how to snatch myself loose of the mental lock that he has over me

constantly fighting off the hands that have touched my spirit
wanting to walk in the healing process, but terrified to go near it
he should be the one who has to battle and struggle and fight
for all the freedom and inner smiles that he has stolen from my life
I have to rally for my own deliverance from the jail he's put me in
desperately waiting for the day when I'll feel less inhibited in my own skin
wanting to be both more and less than what he has deposited in my soul
more than worthless and no good, less than the guilt and shame that I hold

constantly fighting off the hands that have touched my heart's core
and each time I try extending love I am engaged in a tug of war
an intense desire to open up to love and all that it has
an intense fear because of what an open heart has felt like in the past
unable to trust good feelings, unwilling to take that chance
wondering if for the rest of my life I'll be fighting off the hands
fighting off the hands that have touched my mind, spirit and heart's core
constantly fighting for the day when I will not have to fight anymore

Myla Denise

the cell

I can't believe you are responsible
for the negative thoughts that torment me
making it seemingly impossible
for me to ever feel normal or free
what's worse is that while I have to fight
so hard just to functionally maintain
you get to just go on with your life
when your deeds are the cause of my pain
how is it the least bit just
you commit the crime, but I have to pay
your actions have impacted me so much
I have to struggle with this everyday
people even ask me for your name
and I refuse to say anymore
putting you first and that's a shame
but I was never put first before
it's not enough that you stole what you stole
you took my persona and minimized it
memories forever haunting my soul
snatching my peace of mind and parts of my spirit
and I don't know how to cease
to let myself be physically used
putting the needs of others before me
they feel good, I get a new bruise
what am I supposed to do now
I'm stuck in this emotional trap
I've managed to keep smiling somehow
but I can't seem to get beyond that
I don't know how to let myself open up
to acknowledge the depth that I hurt
when I need to talk I keep my mouth shut
rationalizing that talking will just make it worse
and while I do recognize
that I have come a long way
there's still such hurt beneath my eyes
things I can't find adequate words to say
I look at you living well
like you suffered not one consequence
for locking me in this emotional cell
left to wonder if I can ever truly get out of it

Diary Entries

I'm kind of lost. My heart is heavy. There's a level of healing I keep getting really close to getting, but can't get there. I'm sitting just outside of it. I can see it, but I can't touch it. Can't walk in it. I want to get this over with so bad. So bad. The tears are just beyond my eyes, but they won't fall.

****

What happened to me is twisted and sick and sometimes I think that because it happened to me it must define me. I know that's a lie, but it doesn't stop me from thinking it.

*****

The only two people I talk about my past to suggested that I go talk to someone, namely Pastor [Name]. I probably will, but I don't want to disappoint her. Plus, when she asks me if I've been in the word or even consistently praying my answer is no. Then I feel like I'm wasting her time because I haven't done what I need to do. I used to do it that way, but I seemed to be proclaiming healing out of faith and not because I seemed to be getting anywhere. I felt like I was living a lie, professing healing and feeling defeated.

*****

I had my first group therapy session today. It went ok. Suddenly I don't feel so all alone.

Myla Denise

Hold Me

Loving arms try to embrace me and cover me in healing
and I accept the physical touch, but ignore the threat of feeling

not sure if I can handle being so vulnerable and so exposed
because the act of touching previously required my heart to be closed

desperately needing and yet despising the very thing that will set me free
all because I don't know how to let anybody hold me

Diary Entries

My relationship with God is so not around. I've just become numb. Last night to celebrate graduation I got drunk. Before the night ended I got really emotional. Someone was talking about losing her virginity and how old she was. All eyes turned to me because in all the time I'd been living here, no one knew a thing about my life. They asked me if I was a virgin and I said yes and no. I don't know why I said that. I should have just said yes. That first time wasn't my choice. I'm sure it was the alcohol, but I broke down and cried in the bathroom. I sometimes think that I want to cry and have someone hold me and listen to me. Is that childish? I want to be able to let it all out, have someone there to listen and hold me. No more vodka for the kid. I was a mess.

*****

I'm not doing so well today. I had a dream last night. I know they were on my mind last night because I rewrote my poem from November 9, [1999]. While I was recopying it I felt myself holding my jaws real tight so I knew I was getting real angry about it. The dream was quite explicit and when I woke up I felt awful. Right now I don't feel too good either. I feel like they've taken advantage of me time and time again and today is one of those days. I could literally feel him touching me in this dream and I sat there pretending I wasn't there.

I feel like they've taken enough from me as it is. They've taken my childhood, my innocence, many of my good days - much too much to be taking my present, too. And definitely too much to be included in my future. I know I've come a long way, but I'm beginning to wonder if this is as far as I'm going to get. I just want to crawl in bed and cry.

****

I had a disturbing dream while sleeping in the very same bed that I'd been in approached many years ago. I had to pretend like everything was fine, but once I got to my own house I broke down. As I thought about all the times that people violated me my stomach got queasy and I felt like I was going to throw up. I physically felt like it was happening all over again. [My friend] called and I tried to ignore how I felt, but I couldn't. She told me to stand up, but I couldn't move. She only hung up the phone with me so that I could pray and while I prayed I felt instructed to tell God what happened. While I was telling him, I kept hearing, "I was there."

invaded

it's been exhausting to free myself from your grip
and all that you've done that pulled at my spirit
and it's not enough to consciously decide
that I will not give you the power of my present life
because somehow you've been allowed to seep
into my unconscious and disturb my sleep
and it angers me because I have fought so intensely
to keep you from having a hold on me mentally
and to have you invading a time when I should be at peace
feels like an attack on the very center of my being
I don't know how to shake these images that never were
and I question how they can cause such hurt
but I guess it represents so much of what you stole
my peace of mind, security and the feeling of control
in these visions you inhabit sacred spaces
and torment me in the most mundane places
when I wake up my security is unsure
and I don't know what to do anymore
you've taken enough from me, don't you think
why should you be allowed to enter my dreams
but then again you've never really been the type
to ask for permission or be polite
you've just invaded, gone where you didn't belong
then forced me into it, made me come along
I'm tired of you being where you're not invited or asked
I'm tired of you dragging me through the pits of the past
you've taken enough from me, let me go
you've been around far too long and entirely too close
I cannot have this, I must draw the line
you've already invaded my body, I can't give you my mind

Diary Entries

I feel worse than I've felt in a long time. I'm so tired. It's already unfair that I had to go through it, but having to live with it day after day is starting to wear me down. I'm not as strong as I thought I was or maybe my expectations are too high. Is it realistic to think that I'll never think of that ever again? That's what I'd love to do, just never think of it. Like my mind to be wiped clean of all that.

I'm so disappointed in myself for being so weak. Why should events from ten years ago still upset me to such a large degree? It should just be an afterthought like, Oh yeah that happened. No more than that. Instead it totally knocks me over and makes seeing people, having people look in my eyes, so hard. I fear someone just seeing through my smiles and calling me out. That's why I feel so bad when I hear people tell me I'm so strong. They don't see me at home. I wonder how long I'll have to live like this.

As I think about it, something stands out to me. When I feel extremely bad, I almost regress to this infant behavior. I talk so people can hardly hear me and that's only when someone else initiates the conversation. My responses are five words or less. And all I want to do is sit up under someone. I don't do it, but it's what I want. It's like I want to be held. Not in a romantic way, but in a protected fashion. Like I care and I'm not going to let this happen to you again. I still feel like that scared little girl and I'm waiting for someone to protect me. I'm waiting for someone to protect me from my own thoughts.

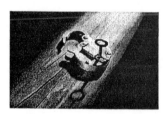

The Worst Thing

Diary Entries

I look at my life and I'm a little disappointed in how I've behaved, as if I'm not anointed. I've allowed myself to be influenced instead of being the one to make the impact. And I'm upset with me because I know better than that. I'm not walking in the wisdom I've struggled to obtain and then I question why it's so hard for me to maintain.

*****

There is so much I want to say, but I'm having a hard time finding the words. I have never felt such distress before. I wake up everyday hoping that today will be a good day. That today my past will not run me over. I know I smile, but sometimes I do it to prevent people from asking questions. Lately I've been pulling away from people. The time I've spent talking to people has allowed me to let out more than ever, but there is still so much inside of me and it hurts not to be able to share. It also hurts holding all this in. I am confident that this will not last forever. But right now I feel pain. Some days I hurt so much I get dizzy.

*****

I was sending an email about [my exboyfriend] and I thought to say, "He made me feel much lower than I should feel." What I typed was, "He made me feel much lower than I already know I am." Was that a slip up?

*****

While I spent time with my parents today I felt like I wanted to say so much. I feel like they don't really know me. My dad expressed an interest in writing a book after I told him that I write. He has no idea of the book that would come out of my heart. It's very strange to think that I come from them and they don't know me. I suppose it's partially my fault because I half explain my visions, desires and fears. My ultimate goal is not to be some famous, rich businesswoman, but it is to be someone influential in improving the lives of people. I want my story told so that others can be inspired and my own father has no idea of what my story is.

Dawn: Diary of a Poet

Something To Tell You

I have something to tell you and it's going to break your heart
the mere thought of this conversation has been extremely hard
once I let you know, I'm sure you will be curious
about the when, why, how and who was doing this
and I have to be selfish for once and make this request
that you just listen to me and not even go through that
I'm only revealing this much so that you'll be prepared
for where I am going before I get there
my purpose in life is to represent
those who have gone where I went
I have to let them know that life is still worth living
that there are still some chances worth taking and giving
and to be a true example the only way I can understand
is to have gone where they are and stood where they stand
you're probably wondering what all of this
has to do with what I want to admit
I'm trying to tell you that these feelings I've described
come right out of the pages of my life
I know what it's like to live under the illusion
that life only brings more hurt confusion
I've felt like I was put here to suffer
and to unwillingly provide myself to others
I've felt like taking a last breath was the only way to attain peace
from all the memories that were hounding me
and the reason I've felt that way I'm not going to explain
or go into details or give up any names
I can only pray that you'll find some kind
of peace knowing I made it out in my right mind
because if I told you the story and how it started
I'm sure that you would be brokenhearted
I have to be selfish and leave the story incomplete
I'm not going back there just to cure curiosity
so I hope you'll understand and fulfill my wish
of letting it go and leaving it at this

Diary Entries

[My friend] told me that she prays I haven't given up on the book idea and that I work on it everyday, even it's just a sentence. I am afraid to even consider beginning. If I finish, well, when I finish, then I'll have to deal with other issues like my family finding out. That book, my book, is going to hurt so many people. I wish there was some way I could publish it anonymously, but still have a way for those who need to contact me to contact me. I know I can't have both. But I'm so concerned with what people will think I'm afraid to even begin. How do you tell your family that you were sexually abused by the family? How do you then explain that you waited until you were in your twenties to mention it? There's my grandparents. My brother and sister. Aunts, uncles. Then there's them. Will they hate me?

*****

I read an article today that mentioned Habbakuk 2:2-3. I love those verses. They are great. "Write down the vision and make it plain...For the vision awaits an appointed time...and will not prove false. Though it lingers, wait for it; it will certainly come and will not delay." I will wait for it.

*****

I've figured out why these dreams bother me as much as they do. The dreams always take place in either the present or the future, as in things that could still happen. I know that God is in complete control of my life, but he was in complete control when I was 5, 6, 7 and so on. All between that time he was in control and I was taken advantage of. How can I be sure that it will never happen again? Especially when I have nearly asked for it recently. I remember thinking that I could not possibly go public because it happened so long ago, but almost hoping one of them would try it again so I could go public now. Now that it is my greatest fear - that I'll be violated again.

Dawn: Diary of a Poet

Buried Alive

I'd like to think I'm easy to get along with
but now I'm starting to have my doubts
my act of constant bliss is wearing thin
and my internal swaying mood I can do without

I've started to live solely for my dreams
ignoring what I feel at times
not at all as together as it seems
or owning up to the emotion that's mine

then there's a point when someone will ask
how I am and I'll flat out lie or downplay
that I need to talk or that I'm sad
and I'm afraid and don't know what to say

the cycle just repeats and I internalize
all emotion waiting for the day to arrive
when my heart will finally realize
that I've held too much in and buried myself alive

Diary Entries

Support group went well today. I just thought it's kind of hard to get such deep and emotional revelations and then be expected to continue the day like nothing happened. I leave there and then go on to class like I hadn't just been discussing the worst part of my life.

We discussed spontaneous age regression and coping strategies. I felt a sense of commonality after one of the girls mentioned that she's seen the guy since it happened. I've generally felt alone in having to see those people and not feel any anger towards them. I've been more angry at someone else. The one that should have responded and protected me.

The weird thing about group is that I don't want it to end. When it's time, I don't want to leave. I wish we met more often. There's an unspoken understanding there and I need that.

*****

Group went well today. I sound like I'm talking about an addicts meeting or something. Anyway, the thing I got out of it was that I've been wrong about my perspective. I felt like feeling sad about my experiences was a way to give all of those people more of me, more than they already took. So instead of allowing myself to feel anything I'd bury my emotions. "They're not getting anymore anything from me!" Sheila said that I should think of it as giving myself time to heal in order to decrease the time I give to them suppressing everything.

I love going to group. I learn so much from listening. They've been called too sensitive, they've felt unworthy of the same things other people take for granted like love and happiness, they have that love/hate war going on inside their hearts regarding their abusers. That sense of commonality helps.

An Old Debt

my intimate moments with men
cause me great distress within
an inactive participant in my heart
only my body is playing the part
rationalizing to get through these dealings
just sit there and let him get his feelings
it will be over sooner if you comply
things are easier and faster if you don't fight
and then I realize I've gone back in time
it's the present, but the past in my mind
I've generalized all situations like this
things have changed, this isn't the same, but I haven't noticed
I know I'm not required to do anything
that the one who finally has control is me
but I can't get out of the mind set of that little girl
where compliance and secrecy were the center of her world
wondering how long life will be this way
how long I'll feel guilty and make myself pay
then it hits me, I'm so conflicted within
because I'm mad at myself for ceasing to fight back then
if I stopped fighting then why should I do it now
the need for me to fight back was more when I was a child
I'm charging myself for an old debt and repeatedly paying the price
for not acting like an adult during my childhood life
and making myself pay for this old debt has made me regress
feeling like a helpless child again, that little girl I can't forget

Diary Entries

It's a little after two and I'm still awake. I've had that all too familiar feeling in my stomach. I wish those thoughts never bothered me again. But it hurts. It hurts for me to think about that confused and scared little girl who got sexual advances from the same people that were supposed to love her. How do you tell someone something that's going on in your life that you don't even have the vocabulary for? And how is that little girl supposed to grow up and act like she's normal? How can I talk to people when I can't even point out what's bothering me? Well, let's see, I've been fondled and screwed before I had my first kiss. It hurts real bad. I wish I could just start over. Maybe if I would have had the courage to speak out before it got so bad I wouldn't be feeling so used, betrayed and just devastated. And even still, I can't cry. Not because it shows a sign of weakness, but because it's a loss of control. I can't lose control. Sometimes I feel like that's all I've got. I'm very disappointed in myself right now. This should be over with. How long will I be upset by an old offense? It's time to move on.

*****

I'm not feeling too well. I feel like something is being pulled out of me and I don't want it to come out. Last night I had trouble sleeping. I feel real scared right now. I was trying to be my silly self earlier, but I had to just leave because I couldn't do it. I'm tired of feeling bad about this. People have always led me to believe that because I still have problems with it I haven't given it to God. But in reading books and listening to people speak I often hear that they still have 'those' days. I've always had the assumption that once I gave it to the Lord it wouldn't bother me anymore. Maybe I was just wrong in assuming such. All I can ask for right now is guidance when I have one of those days so that I can handle it in a better way. Is this really something that will effect me forever?

*****

I always think about those times whenever I sleep in a new place. I just can't help but think about the open door or simply being in a different bed. I'm in Miami, supposed to be enjoying myself. It was a little easier because [my friend] was in the room with me. I thought about waking her to tell her how I was feeling, but I decided against it. I'm tired of talking about it, remembering it or feeling uncomfortable when I hear the words rape, molestation or sexual abuse. I am not sure why, but hearing those words made me uncomfortable and made me ask myself, "Is that you?" or "Did that really happen?" How is it possible that something that happened so long ago manages to still make me sick to my stomach? And will I have these moments for the rest of my life?

Dawn: Diary of a Poet

How Long

How long will my opinion of myself depend
on how I think others perceive me or on the words of my friends
How long will I allow myself to silently endure
reflections of a past that causes emotional torture
How long will I lie to myself and pretend myself behind a look
telling myself not to be impacted though my foundation's been shook
How long will I smile and say that I am fine
when I'm so unsure of myself so much of the time
How long will I beat up on myself for trying to live a normal life
refusing to release by adamantly fighting urges to cry
How long will I deny myself the right to be upset
in all these years I still can't embrace my true feelings yet
How long will I scold myself saying it's been long enough
so compassionate towards others and on myself so tough
How long will I continue to stand in my own way
reaching out to be freed, but keeping the healing process at bay
running back every time I feel uncomfortable or start to hurt too much
wanting God's healing yet frightened of the power of his touch
afraid that if I totally give up control my emotions will be too strong
and he's waiting patiently, asking me the same question, how long?

Diary Entries

My prayer life leaves so much to be desired. I think part of me has been afraid to really tap into the Lord like I used to. There's a place in me that is afraid to expose all of me. He has healed me in pieces, how do I know that the next healing won't break me into pieces?

*****

I'm just getting back from group and it was hard to sit through today. We discussed the difference between guilt and shame. Guilt involves feeling bad about an action or a thought. Shame is feeling bad about self. I feel both.

Then we discussed seduction and threat. I got a threat, not from them, but from those who were supposed to protect me. One girl talked about her mom who acts like she has nothing to do with it and how she couldn't imagine how much her lack of action/emotion impacts this girl's life. I can relate, but I even feel guilty about that.

*****

Group was a little intense. The physiological effects of being abused. We were stimulated too early. I always struggle with that. It makes so much sense in my head, like much of this stuff, but learning to truly accept it in my soul is a little harder. We talked about being that silent child so that no one notices us. I've done that so often, tried to fit into the background so no one pays much attention to me. What's ironic is while I was trying to go unnoticed I still wanted someone to help me, to rescue me. I wanted someone to notice me hiding and help.

I wrote a poem called Memories and it is so true of how I feel. I wish my memories weren't mine. If my calling was to help the brokenhearted, why did I have to have it so extreme? Why not just one person? What did it have to be both sexes for? Why did it have to be family members? I have to live with their reactions and it bothers me. I don't want to hurt anybody.

Dawn: Diary of a Poet

Memories

I keep wishing my memories didn't belong to me
their severity and content leave me in disbelief
wondering how I got dealt so many blows
and the extent of it all, no one really knows
I never would have wished for any part of this
but if confronting such a monster was just my gift
how come it had to be in addition to such complexity
numerous offenders, both sexes, all people in my family
confusion compacted upon confusion
leading me to desire that it was all an illusion
that my memories were only twisted imaginations
and that the hurt in my heart was just an imitation
it's easier for me to accept that my mind betrayed me
than to fully grasp the concept that someone raped me
easier to think that it was all a dream that never took place
than to admit what is always just beneath the smile on my face
having some part of this with me everywhere I go
triggered by a scene in a movie or a comment on the radio,
or an article in a magazine or watching the news on tv
everything that I do has the potential to remind me
that I'm that one out of four, or that twenty-fifth percent
and I hate that I'm on that side of the statistic
sometimes I feel as if I'd rather go out of my mind
than to acknowledge that the memories I have really are mine
that they aren't simply fabricated and they aren't just crazy thoughts
I'd rather disown my retention than pay what it costs
but that option is not mine to decide
I can only choose to live or to slowly die
and as hard as it is to repeatedly see
the scenes that threaten to suffocate me
I know there's a reason why my life has been kept
and the fullness of it all I may not even recognize yet,
I just have to tell myself that my memories are images of a time that is over
and done
and they don't dictate where I'm going, they only tell what I've overcome

Diary Entries

I found this scripture today. Love it. Proverbs 10:7 says the memory of the righteous will be a blessing. God is creating new memories for me that will be a blessing. My last memories will be, at the very least, a blessing. That encouraged me so. I love how the Lord uses the word to give me hope, joy and smiles.

*****

One of the most prominent things I heard in group today was that we're trying to reconstruct that sense of security and we do that by performing. Dr. A said that we saw we weren't protected by being so we figured it was by doing. That is so me. I've felt that in order to keep people in my life I have to do something for them. It's not enough to simply be me.

*****

In group today Dr. A explained what happens when a child's needs aren't met. It was quite deep. She said if an infant never gets her needs met she learns that the world doesn't provide. If an infant cries out of fear and instead gets a bottle, she may be taught that she can't trust her own feelings or that when she's scared she's supposed to eat. I don't know what I was taught. I can't believe group will be over in a week. Where do I go from here? What am I supposed to do when this is over? I feel exposed and like I'm being thrown back too soon.

the worst thing

people say that the worst thing that can happen to victims would be
for them to tell their story and then not be believed
but what happens when you tell the story and it's recognized as true
and then the suggested course of action revolves around what not to do
implying that it's not important for you to heal yourself
because the most important thing is not to tell anyone else
I think I would have preferred it if I wouldn't have been believed
then I wouldn't have had to find out that my well-being was not the priority

Diary Entries

She walked in once while he was on top of me. A seven year old girl with her dress pulled up. I try to change the ending of my memory, but it never changes. She didn't do anything.

*****

I got this book, The Wounded Heart. I flipped through the pages. I still can't believe I bought the thing. I read the acknowledgments. That was easy enough. Just a bunch of people the author had to thank. I read the foreword just to avoid getting into the real reading. In the second paragraph were words I didn't want to see yet. That was supposed to be in the real book. If I wanted to see all this about molestation I would have started on the real book. I needed baby steps. It was traumatic enough for me to buy the thing. I didn't want the girl who rang me up to read the cover. I imagined her trying to say something polite to me. Just to be nice to the girl who needed the sexual abuse book.

I flung the book on my bed a little harder than I meant to. I watched it bounce off the mattress and hit the floor with a thud. It amused me for some reason. I started to just leave it there. That's where it could stay as far as I was concerned. That's the only place I could stand it if it had to stay in my apartment. It might as well be on the floor, where I put my feet. Where I can walk on it. Like I've walked on everything else concerning that part of my life.

Why I Fight

Diary Entries

My eyes have been tearing up all day, but the tears wouldn't fall, probably because I wouldn't let them. It's strange - the same situation that encourages me and lets me know how far I've come is the same one that really hurts my heart and keeps me from moving forward. I try to convince myself that this is all a process, but I can't help feeling like I'm taking two steps forward and one step back. Knowing that I'm still moving forward is encouraging, but I can't help getting frustrated for going so slow.

*****

How can I be so positive about my future and yet I want to cry over my present?

*****

I have to write this book. The number of people that it will hurt will be significantly less than the number of people that it will help. I considered leaving out the parts concerning my mother's reaction, but I feel any lesson I learned that I purposely left out will be unfair. There may be someone out there who feels unsupported too and I can't leave them feeling alone about an experience that I also had. That would defeat the purpose - helping others and self release.

I just got the answer to the prayer I've been praying for years. When I've heard, 'Just release it,' that meant write the book, not just let it go. The best way to express appreciation for answered prayer is to proceed without doubt. My book will help to heal others, but it will also release me. I don't normally release my emotions through tears, I do so by writing so why should this release be any different? I shall release myself through writing. Not only that, but writing a book to inspire others too. My life is ordered by God even when I don't recognize it.

*****

I want to work in a profession where I help people open up when I can't open up either. If I could, I would tell people that it hurts. It hurts to have the memories I have, to love the people I'm supposed to be so angry with. It hurts to smile in my family's face knowing that I've kept an entire part of my life a secret. It hurts to be on this roller coaster of emotions all by myself. Knowing that I'm seemingly in this alone and that I will continue to be for a while longer hurts, too.

Dawn: Diary of a Poet

Because I Have To

I don't think that people understand me
they don't see how I remain encouraging and upbeat
some think that I'm not completely honest
one who ignores her feelings because of this
but the truth is when depression threatens to run me down
when fear and memories try to slap me around
I do what I must to make it through
basically, I keep smiling because I have to

how much easier it would be
to simply let sadness overtake me
that doesn't require any effort, I'd just sit
and let myself fall into a self-pity pit
true, when you're down there's nowhere to look but up
but what happens if while I'm down I just keep my eyes shut
I'd get accustomed to darkness and solitaire
eventually losing both the ability and desire to care

I know I don't want that for myself, I want more
so I hold it together, constantly trying to close that door
because I know that if I let myself go down that road
I'll fall so far I won't be able to get out on my own
I recognize my emotions, but I also realize
that sadness is not a state where I desire to abide
I'll continue my battle and keep my upbeat attitude
and I'll keep smiling, basically, because I have to

Diary Entries

I'm kind of glad I've started to tell people I was molested. Now I feel like I can be myself. Not saying that I've been fake, I've just been hiding a part of myself. I wish I could tell what happened without telling who did it.

*****

I'm reading the Wounded Heart and I see more of myself than I want. Yet at the same time, I don't feel like such a unique case. The author touched on how many are abused by more than one person. That added to my shame because I was the common denominator. It had to be my fault. Something I did. Then he mentioned the betrayal felt by being unprotected. Not only during, but after. It's no secret to me that a lack of action from people caused me to feel and question quite a bit. I already know that whatever in life that could have destroyed me can be the very thing that leads to making my life great.

Living with what I've lived with has increased my capacity to love, to feel and to believe in my strength. Because of my experiences I'm in a place that gives me credibility to encourage people. I'm not encouraged by people that have never gone through anything. And I'm sure I'm not the only person who feels that way. My goodness. When I consider the possibilities... When I think about all the people I have the potential to inspire... God is so good. I am so thankful. This life is so much bigger than me and my feelings. I have an assignment and I will carry it out.

It hurt, it still hurts. More hurt is probably to come, but now, I know it will all be worth it in a little while. I don't want to miss out.

Diary Entries

I've said it before, but I truly wish my abusers weren't in my family. I wish I could just say it was someone else, someone no longer in my life. That'd make it a little simpler. At least I wouldn't feel bad about telling. I'm not telling to punish anybody, but to free somebody.

*****

I can feel myself wanting to pull away from my family. I do need to be a bit more strengthened, but part of it is guilt. Knowing what is about to go down. Knowing that what I'm about to reveal is going to break their hearts. And I'm acting as if all is well. Not that I'm having second thoughts. I'm going to do this. I owe it to God. I owe it to myself. I owe it to all those people who need to hear my story. I just think about how my family will react. Not that I have any control over that, but I do think about it. I really just want to get this over with.

*****

I Need You Now by Smokie Norful just came on the radio. How appropriate. I thank God for being faithful to me, especially in the many times where I wasn't faithful to myself. Every time I look into my father's face I feel like I'm living a lie. I'm not the daughter he knows. And I dread the day when he finds out the truth. I dread it for him, but I need it for me. I know that once I tell him I can tell anybody. My freedom is coming. My prayer is that he and the rest of my family will respect my wishes and try not to bombard me with a million questions.

Myla Denise

Two Paths

I see two paths before me
the first requires that I commit spiritual suicide
all the secrets on the edge of my tongue, I bite
they poison my soul then leave me empty
and I'm sentenced to a life of settling and pretending
settling for a future that is greatly diminished
pretending that my testimony is smaller than it is
neglecting those who need to hear how I was freed
because they are on the same path not too far behind me

The second path frightens me to immobility
just the mere idea of opening my mouth and exposing
having to live with my loved one's reactions
and countless questions about what happened
the potential for division and many accusations
people unable to see past their anger and speculations
leaving me in the middle of a war where I start as the center
eventually forgotten because everyone is too busy pointing the finger

Which path will I choose?
What should I do?
Condemn myself to silence
or condemn my family with the news?
But why should I keep it?
Wouldn't that imply
that I've done something wrong
or that I have something to hide?
people are quick to say
it's not my fault and if that's true
I should not force myself to keep this in
And have a self-sabotaging attitude
and what about all those people
who need to follow my lead?
I can't be responsible for deceiving
or causing them more misery
I no longer see two paths before me
for the path of silence is not mine to take
I hope my family will forgive me
because I must follow the road to faith

Diary Entries

My next question is how do I tell the family. Do I just let them read the book? Do I sit everybody down? Do I write a letter? I truly do not know what to do or how to handle this. I will simply trust God. That's all I can do. He's gotten me this far. I thought about telling [my aunt] first, but I don't think I'm ready for a one-on-one with anybody. I'd feel better in a less confrontational prone environment. Not trying to have a question and answer session. Maybe I should write a letter. Tell everybody that the subject matter of my books and poems might be disturbing, but what's important is that I am OK. But I don't have to completely clown. This book might not be out for a while. This book could be several years away. God will direct my path. No worries.

*****

I feel bad because the bliss of ignorance is coming to an end soon. After the holidays I have to tell [my dad] the truth. Another year can't pass like this. Plus, Dawn has to come out. It's time. I can't halt my success, God's plans for my life and the healing process of others because of one single conversation. That's not logical.

****

To get myself together I must set myself apart.

Myla Denise

The Little Girl

I look into the face of this little girl and her eyes convey
everything she feels, but cannot find the words to say
her hair wears a fresh press, her outfit is too cute
at a glance, her million dollar smile says, there's nothing I can't do
but looking a little closer, searching beyond that precious grin
I see secrets that this child keeps deep within
there lies fear of being her true self, thinking she's not enough
times she's wanted to speak up for herself, but she kept her mouth shut
she would constantly compare herself to how pretty the other little girls were
never thinking people would use a word like that to describe her
feeling inferior, but putting on an air of false confidence
so no one would notice or make her admit to it
I tremble as I realize I'm looking at her twenty years later
how can a mere image of her affect my behavior
maybe because it's not a picture, it is a reflection that I see
in the mirror, in those eyes, that little girl is looking back at me

Dawn: Diary of a Poet

My Choice

I've had to live with your decision as if it were mine
this single nightmare has lasted me my lifetime
sometimes I want to ask how you could do what you did
how could you steal my womanhood while I was yet a kid
but you were young too so I wonder if you realize
just how much your actions have affected my life
that's why it's especially hard, I would love to just hate you
but I'm not even sure you understand all that I've gone through
all because of your decision to leave me without a choice
because you deemed me unworthy of having a voice
I've had to erase all of the lessons I learned from you
because when you took what you stole, you deposited some things too
my anchor became guilt and shame
making me think it was my fault my heart held such pain
made me feel unimportant, like I didn't matter much
which led to others being able to subject me to that familiar touch
I put up a fight at first, but that didn't last
I remembered how unsuccessful my fighting had been in the past
and I thought my whole purpose in life was to bring pleasure to everyone else
without a word of complaint and at the expense of myself
but I know better now and I'm working to unlearn what your lessons taught
by using to my advantage all the negativity that your actions brought
I'm going to make it my life's mission to be a catalyst
for those who've been where I've been and need an advocate
and while it may never occur to you the damage you've done completely
I have a choice now and you will no longer have a hold on me

Diary Entries

I need to lean on my own strength and as the song says, I need to find my 'strength in love.' Love for myself. For this week I'm going to try speaking less. I have this idealistic view of relationships and how they should go and lately those expectations have been getting me in trouble, really hurt. I just want people to make good on what they say. "If you ever need me...if you ever want to talk...you can always come to me...I'm always here for you..." I'm finding out that's not true. People should say, "I'm always there as long as..." As long as it's convenient for me. As long as my own life isn't too pressing. As long as you don't really need me. I never tell anybody when I really need them.

*****

Life doesn't stop to check on me. I have to roll with it or get rolled over.

*****

Today wasn't my best. I was sad and I don't even know why or what triggered it. Quiet and queasy all day. I attribute this to a growth spurt or something. I know one thing, I must stop beating up on myself. It's ridiculous. I get mad at myself for holding so much in, but then more upset when I need to talk. It's crazy.
I will get through this. The worst is over. It's over. It's all over.

*****

I saw the words it's not your fault. Every time I hear or see that I think, "I know, but still." Still I find myself asking was it really theirs? Whose fault was it truly?

Dawn: Diary of a Poet

The Familiar Stranger

you are a familiar stranger
I don't know you by name
but I'm well-acquainted with your actions
and all the repercussions that came
you are the most dangerous type of predator
causing your prey to pounce
on each other while you are the culprit
yet your identity never comes out

the more I get through this healing process
the more I understand
that those who hurt me were just repeating acts
they suffered by your hands
you taught them to be abusers
when you showed them how to be abused
these children followed your example
and I became the next muse

the faces I've associated with my pain
the ones I've directed all of the blame
are not solely responsible for much of my heartbreak
for that I have you to thank
even though I don't know who you are
I know that this extends far beyond
those who directly inflicted hurt on me
those I'd previously placed all the anger upon

I don't know your identity
and I'm sure you don't know how much
the effects of what you did
went far beyond the ones you touched
what I experienced was part of an ugly circle
and I'm not sure if you were the initiator
but I'm cutting it off and calling you out
I'm choosing to be more powerful than an imitator

I will not shut up about it
I refuse to be a spineless casualty
this cycle has to end
so I'm putting you on notice publically
I will write about it until my heart is freed
I will inspire until my mind is clear

Myla Denise

there's a contract out on the death you spread
the end of your destruction in my life is near
I wouldn't have wished to be in this place,
but since you put me in this position
I will gladly fight this fight
as healing heartbreak has become my mission

Diary Entry

I've always wondered what kind of person I would have been if I never was 'approached' by all those people. I now realize that I was born to encourage and I will still encourage people despite the abuse. Maybe even more because of it. I would not be a different person. I am and have always been what God intended me to be.

Myla Denise

Diminished

I would love to be myself, but I'm not always sure who that is
because I think that who I was born to be was diminished when I was a kid
so many tried to dim my light that I'm afraid to let it shine
and the guilt or shame that should have latched onto to them has become mine
my voice often gets caught in my throat and in the event that it escapes
it's usually in a tone where I'm actually sorry for having something to say
moments alone in prayer reveal that there still remains greatness inside
not allowed to be snuffed out or snatched because it's an internal light
with the Lord on the inside of me my greatness cannot be diminished
the greatness I desire to reach will not be until God is finished
no one has ever made me any less than what the Lord intended
because no one has that kind of power over me unless I permit it

Dawn: Diary of a Poet

why I fight

flat on my face, down on my knees
asking if God can hear or see me
my heart hurts, I feel so alone
want to reach out, but can't pick up the phone
and where I thought I'd always depend
is gone because I'm not totally honest with friends
the ones I thought would forever be there
are the very same ones I've left so unaware
no idea of what's going on with me
because when we catch up I'm always pretending
giving the impression that all I possess
is a positive attitude and the secret to happiness
never fully opening up or letting people in
not sure if I can or where I would even begin
lately my mood has started to fluctuate
and how I feel just depends on the day
while I am excited and confident about my life
sure that I'll be an author in due time
I still have moments when I seriously wonder
if my emotions will one day take me under
and I have plenty of insecure days
negative thoughts and self-isolating ways
I've heard I need to talk, just let it all out
but I am sick of talking, I'll just go another route
I want God to just remove this load off me
just erase all this hurt miraculously
I'm tired of working so hard at dealing with my past
especially when I don't know how long this mess will last
and working through all this emotion is no guarantee
that I'll ever truly get over my hurt and memories
I could fight my entire life and it could still elicit hurt
then I'd have to ask myself why I even bothered with that work
but part of me knows the answer to that, even before I ask
part of me knows why I've hidden behind a mask
in my heart I am aware that my life fulfillment
comes from encouraging other people, I smile for their benefit
if I can uplift others and help them to more joyously live
then I'll be satisfied knowing I gave all I could give

The Other Side of Blue

Diary Entry

I just thought about how I'm at the same house I had some of the biggest laughs and also felt so terrible. The same house where I've felt so much love is the same house where I've felt such deep betrayal. While I've forgiven, I can't forget. I used to think that I couldn't forget because it happened so often - that's not why. I can't forget because of what happened, not because of how many times it happened. Sometimes it baffles me how much I experienced and I'm really OK. My life is going great. I still have growing up to do, issues to resolve, but for my age I am doing pretty well.

The Other Side of Blue

with smiling eyes I realize that I'm feeling kind of blue
not an overwhelming feeling, it's a subtle kind of mood
not sad or lonely or longing for anyone or anything
to be in my blue mood puts my mind at ease
a sense of peace and tranquility floods over me as calm as a stream
as gentle and comforting as the sound of a small, trickling creek
it's a deep turquoise and teal blue, one of serenity
as refreshing as an autumn night rain would be
this isn't a new place for me, it's more like deja vu
back to where I like to be, on the other side of blue

Myla Denise

Diary Entries

Today I need to forgive myself. I've felt guilty for a long time for placing a name and a face on my abuser, particularly [his name]. While what I said was the truth, I felt guilty for telling on him. I say that because he wasn't the only one. I've never volunteered the names of the others, but I have told people his name and I have felt bad about that.

*****

I looked in the mirror and I saw myself just lunge out at myself. I beat up on myself constantly for not being over the abuse. If I had compassion on myself like I do my friends I would be fine.

42

Dawn: Diary of a Poet

Mirror

I used to look in mirrors and see an empty void, no emotion
fearful that if I allowed myself to feel, I'd get knocked over
one day I walked by a mirror and God turned on the light
I couldn't look long, it hurt too much so I shielded my eyes
so God sent people to tell me what I refused to see
positive affirmations and I was convinced they couldn't mean me
their uplifting words fell on deaf ears
figured they were lying, I chose not to hear
so God sat me down and forced me to face
the truth about my life, even what I tried to erase
took me to the beginning, to a place and a time
where it seemed impossible for me to find peace of mind
getting external messages telling me what I wasn't worth
reinforcing that people would only provide more hurt
experienced ugly things so I thought ugly was my definition
negativity blinded me so that my own face was beyond my recognition
various people treated me worthless so I figured I must be
then told me not to speak up so I kept it all inside me
so many secrets left to haunt and torment my heart
shut me up, beat me down then tear me apart
broke down my self esteem before I could even
look to myself and start to believe in
my worth, that I had beauty, a purpose and a fate
too many harmful lessons latched on along the way
I had more questions than answers, like where was God all those times
that I was repeatedly misused and felt like I would abandon my mind
and what kind of person could I possibly grow up to be
with a childhood that taught so much about unbelief
how can I go on with a foundation so shaken
when my naive expectation about the goodness of life was taken
how can I explain my pain when the main source causes such shame
and what happens when giving the blame to a face and a name
turns into many names, many factors, many reasons
how could I not turn all that to myself and commit internal treason
it must have been my fault, my flaw, my defect
that gave others the right to treat me with such disrespect
so that's why I avoided mirrors, that's where the real blame lies
in my own face, behind my own eyes
but God forced me to look at myself today
removed all distractions so I couldn't look away
and I began to see myself the way that he does
eyes with compassion, kindness, mercy and love

Myla Denise

showing me my power and continuous strength
how I've overcome time and time again
told me that the blame I grabbed such a tight grip on
was never intended for me to take all along
that people could look at me and sincerely see
God's peace, joy and beauty radiating out of me
he showed me his plan and how it was perfectly fulfilled
because the me I see today is the one that's been in his will
so as I look at mirrors now I don't turn away
I slow down, take a long look, smile and say
how thankful I am to God for his mercy and grace
and for finally allowing me to look at myself with a smile on my face

Diary Entry

Maybe I'm not delivered because what I need to do is something I truly don't want to do. When the Lord tells me to let it go I interpret that to mean ignore it. That's not it. Maybe it's time for me to talk this thing out. I'm afraid to talk it out because I don't want anyone to know such details about me, especially people that I care for.

Myla Denise

am I really

am I really so outward serving that I honestly care less
about myself and more about how other people feel
or do I think I'm not deserving of being free and blessed
rather put on a happy face instead of owning up to what I feel
am I really that confident and do I thoroughly savor
being alone and in the company of myself
or do I cherish it because I'm doing myself a favor
if I'm alone I can't be hurt by anyone else
am I really getting closer to an emotional breakthrough
or am I just barely starting to reach beyond
the depth of my anguish, I don't have the slightest clue
and I'm afraid this process has hardly begun
am I really going to have the life I dream of and desire
and be blessed to find inner peace along the way
or will I get the career and become an instant liar
never admitting the pain I have from childhood days
am I really wasting my time asking myself questions
about things I'm not sure I want answers for
or is this the first step in the process of learning my lessons
to take the time to know, respect and love myself more

Diary Entry

Here I am, where I've been before hands upraised, face on the floor I've tried to handle my life without your help never have I felt so by myself so here I am, where I've been before hands upraised, face on the floor God, I need you to help me

Myla Denise

God is Good

the statement God is good is sufficient by itself
it's a complete thought, doesn't require anything else
it's not conditional so it's unnecessary to include
circumstances, situations, moods or attitudes
God is not good only when life looks like
it is in your favor or when you feel everything is tight
God is not good only during Sunday morning praise
when the choir's in your ear and the preacher's in your face
God is good all the time and that is not reflective
of the consequences of our choices or our own perspective
sometimes life becomes less than we expect
because God isn't finished strengthening us yet
other times it's the result of us not living as we should
but no matter what, God is still good

Dawn: Diary of a Poet

I Will Continue

I considered my own mortality
Wondered about my life ending
The thought of finality scared me
My life is seemingly just beginning

So I made myself envision future events
Things I'm positive I'll get to do
Dreams and times God can't let me miss
And I was convinced that I will continue

The Bible says that Christ will be glorified
In either how I live my life or in my death
It's up to me to choose to stay alive
By being his example everyday that I have left

Diary Entries

I've tried to minimize the seriousness of the situation by saying something happened to me. Or I was approached. Approached for what? That sounds more livable than what I'm saying without saying. Never wanting to call it what it is. I was sexually abused. What I lived through was abuse. It really was. Now that I can admit that, I can probably move on. I was abused, but God kept me. I'm still here.

*****

I'd rather inspire than be admired.

*****

My only entry for today is stand.

Dawn: Diary of a Poet

Poem for Candace Cole

I read your story
and I am amazed
at all you experienced
compared to who you are today
Your spirit remained
in spite of all you went through
the rejection, neglect,
emotional, mental and sexual abuse
I'm proud of your courage
and what you decided to do
not only did you fight your way out
now you're helping others too
I'm encouraged by your strength
reminding me that I can overcome
because you've felt what I feel
and what I want in life you've done
I recognize that all the qualities in you
that were intended to be minimized
only became so much more noticeable
and prominent in your life
What was supposed to destroy your character,
your beauty and leave you feeling heartless
has only strengthened you and made
your beautiful heart your most respected characteristic
So if no one has told you today
let me be the one to remind
that you are so appreciated
for being so generous with your life and time
Thank you for being strong enough
to be willing to do God's will
because I know it wasn't easy
and how uncomfortable it made you feel
Thank you for being so unselfish
by telling a story that needed to be told
thank for simply being who you are
and developing into Rev. Candace Cole

Diary Entries

Living without being an inspiration or a source of encouragement is not truly living. I believe we all have the ability to encourage. Some are just too afraid to share. Others are too bitter. I just want to be willing.

*****

Saying that people will better understand me after they find out that I was abused just shows me that I need to work on self-definition. In all honesty, that in no way defines me as person. I am much more than that. All that would tell someone is a part of my past.

Dawn: Diary of a Poet

Smile Through the Visions

I have to smile through the visions of what my life used to consist of
smile through the reminders that I grew up questioning the nature of love
those that were to supposed to protect me either couldn't or didn't do it
those that should been an example to me are the ones who put me through it
I don't know how to invite love, as so-called love used to force its way in
and once I was exposed, it began devouring me from within
latching onto my heart, taunting my existence
threatening to both suffocate and drown me in it
pain in my bloodstream, flowing uninhibited
disrupting my mind, squeezing my heart, conceiving unrest in my spirit
it wants to cut off my air supply, intending to slowly erase my life
trying to take me out with painful jabs, then twisting the knife
everyday that I reject it, it returns with a higher intensity
its hunger not satisfied until it finishes me off completely
it's not enough that I've been diminished and my mind has permanently etched
images of the sordid events I beg my heart to forget
I realize that there has to be a reason why this thing fights me so diligently
obviously trying to take me out so I can't share my testimony
so I can't proclaim that God is the only reason why I function and haven't given up
his mercy and grace kept me from addictions of promiscuity, alcohol and drugs
if God didn't strengthen me when I couldn't find the will to live
I never would have found the power that exists in the ability to forgive
if it wasn't for the Lord's comfort my path would have led to a mental facility
I would have willingly gone out of my mind just to escape my aching reality
the Lord held onto me despite my pleas to him to just let me go
teaching me that I have to fight today so I'll have the victory tomorrow
if God hadn't believed in me more than I believed in him
I would have made the choice to stop breathing, I would have let my light dim
if the Lord hadn't loved me sincerely and without conditions
I never would have known that such really existed
God has kept me and through him I can finally experience pure love
and I will continue to smile through the visions of what my life used to consist of

In His Presence

Diary Entries

Think on purpose. Always think on purpose.

*****

I must stay strong enough to let the Lord be my strength.

*****

I heard someone say how she thought it was ironic that she's providing hope to others when life was so hopeless to her years before. I think it's brilliant. Who better to provide hope to the hopeless than someone who has been there? Who better to provide a sense of joy to the depressed than someone who has been there? I know that I can provide inspiration to the brokenhearted because I've experienced it. And I am so grateful to know that there is life after being broken. There is still life after torment. The negative is not the end of the story. The negative is usually the start. My story is not nearly over.

*****

I'm about to increase. My increase in wisdom, guidance and understanding will come from me making the choice to get alone and simply listen. I believe that I have access to all the answers to the questions I have about my life and the direction it's headed, but I must get alone.

Dawn: Diary of a Poet

What You Started

While I'm excited about the direction my life is taking
and thankful to God for all the changes he's making,
I wonder sometimes if I have the strength within
to live in a way that is pleasing to him
he gave me the blueprints and I'm not confident I can
do what I must to live according to his plan
I contemplated packing up my things and running away
not telling a soul and changing my name
that has to be easier than what he's asking of me
that's why I want to ask him to just leave it be
let me live an average life with no extras or extravagance
for the first time in my life, I at least want to have a chance
to live an everyday, normal life like most people can
I'm satisfied with living my life the way that I am
then I'm reminded of that scripture, exceedingly and above
all that I can ask or even think of
and God tells me that those are the very words I've prayed
but now that he's ready to grant my request I am afraid
I feel like I've had more than enough and I'm already satisfied
that I made it through those difficult years and I've survived
I don't want to confront anyone or disperse my pain
and reek havoc in my family while everyone tries to place blame
I don't want to relive those moments just to ease other's curiosity
I don't want to hear, why didn't you say something, why didn't you tell me?
I don't want to have to defend myself in the event that someone lies
I don't want to say those words and then look into my father's eyes
I feel like I've spent more than my soul has in simply trying to live
and press through the mess and keep a smile on my face and constantly forgive
I don't have the energy or even the desire to do this next step
until I hear the slightest whisper ask,

Don't you want to help?
how can you go on knowing that other people can relate
to what you have felt and still sometimes feel and just turn and walk away?
how can you close your heart and not share your history
with those of similar backgrounds who are literally pleading
for just one person to sincerely say, I truly understand
and if I can make it out, then there's no doubt in my mind that you can?
do you really think that you were brought out of such adversity
to keep it to yourself and live a life being average and ordinary?
you have a talent, gift and anointing that is not easily gained

it's not immediately given, it has to be slowly developed and obtained
you've already done the hardest part, that's why I know you'll get through
the toughest task I set before you was for you to edify and affirm you
your purpose is to uplift the down-trodden and inspire the brokenhearted
you are an encourager, don't you want to finish what you started?

Diary Entries

I'm sitting at my dad's. Watching Law and Order. Christmas was beautiful. I'm starting to look at my dad with thoughts like, "It's almost time." I'm ready to tell him. I can't move on with my life, move on with my destiny without freeing myself.

*****

Today began the first day of my life as a free woman. I feel like he sees me through different eyes. Almost like a grown person for real. Like a woman. Or maybe he can see me in the same visionary eyes I've been trying to get him to for so long. I'd love for the Lord to just reveal to my dad the big picture. Just to show him that God is real and maybe reduce the sting a little. My biggest hurdle has been jumped. Praise the Lord, Hallelujah, I'm free!

*****

I've been trying to process the talk I had with my dad and I realize I've been fronting. The truth is I'm thankful for the lack of theatrics, but now I feel like I've traded the source of my shame. What I experienced as a child is no longer holding me captive, but my father's perception of me has grounded and locked me in a web of anger and hurt. I've freed myself from one jail and walked into another. How can I not be hurt when his words suggest that all the pain I've felt was at my own wishes? How can you suggest to a victim of abuse that it wasn't abuse? And how do I live with that?

*****

I've come to understand that the reaction I've received from him possibly came from a stand point of denial. He probably didn't know how to accept what I was saying. It's easier to accept that I wanted it than to accept that I was forced. But where does that leave me? I never had an option to make anything easier. Why should he?

Myla Denise

Trust Me

I get overwhelmed at the thought of my destiny
considering all God has planned, I can't, but think, why me?
surely I'm not the one that is capable to succeed
at all the things he's shown me that he wants me to be
I have serious doubts about my shortcomings and flaws,
my weaknesses, insecurities and emotional pitfalls
he has to be mistaken by giving me such visions
I'm not good enough, there's so much that I'm missing
and how can he possibly consider taking me up
when I have the nerve to question him so much
shouldn't he give these dreams to someone with complete faith
that won't express doubt about his choices along the way
before I can even form these thoughts into a prayer
I hear God ask, "Why are you talking like I'm not there?
I've heard your concerns and here's what I think,
it's time for you to listen to me speak
for you to have this thing called faith, you simply have to believe
I know exactly what I am doing, I just need you to trust me
all of your excuses for being nervous about my design
make you the perfect candidate for what I have in mind
you are simply verbalizing doubt that many people feel
and I need someone exactly like you to show some I am real
if I took your advice and selected only the ones that seem to be
ideal specimens in the eyes of man, who do you think would get the glory?
I take those same ones that man will reject,
ignore, abandon, misuse and disrespect
and I make their lives true examples that all things
are possible and attainable through me
I do this because it's important that people understand
external factors are trivial, I look inside the heart of a man
and I also do it for ones like you who have experienced negativity
for not being what man is so intent on demanding
so by secular standards, you could assume that you are insufficient,
but I've come with a different set of criteria for which you are absolutely perfect
I came that you might have life more abundantly
and that is exactly what you will have, you only need to trust me."

Diary Entries

It's funny to me how life has such wonderful plans for us and instead of working towards that, we think we know what's best and we want God to come down to our level while he's trying to get us to move up to his.

*****

Do it afraid. I keep telling myself that ever since I read it in Joyce Meyer's book Beauty for Ashes. Hopefully, by the time I publish I will no longer be afraid, but if I am, I will do it afraid.

*****

I heard a powerful message from Dr. Showell yesterday. That lady broke it down! She said the Lord was preparing to take us out of great and into greater. That many of us have had great pain, great hurt, but the healing that was coming was going to be greater than the pain and the hurt. She told us we didn't go through for nothing. That the Lord was going to make a billboard out of our lives. I receive that! I am only here and in my right mind because of the saving grace of God. And I don't mind telling it. I will be a billboard for God. I want to be an ad for hope.

*****

God speaks to me constantly, I'm just not constantly listening.

*****

My cross is not too heavy.

3

Myla Denise

Morning Whisper

I'm sitting here watching over you sleep
You look so content and at peace
I'm here because there's a few things I want to say
Before you wake up and begin your day
This morning I wanted to drop something in your spirit
I'm here now hoping that more than your ears would hear it
I hope you fully grasp the entire meaning when I tell you
That the quality of your day depends on what you choose
Ultimately it's up to you to make a conscious decision
That determines the type of everyday life you'll endure living
It begins with your approach, your attitude is a direct reflection
On how you interpret the day's events and your perception
I understand that situations don't always go the way you'd like
But trust, you'll have an easier time if you learn who to fight
You ask for me to intervene and then when I do
My biggest opposition turns out to be you
You either ignore what I say or you fight my plans with a strong fist
And then when enticed or distracted with negativity you hardly even resist
So that's why I catch you early, every morning about this time
Before you've done anything or before everything clutters your mind
Each day hoping that this will be the one that you will decide
To accept my joy, peace and love today and for the rest of your life

Diary Entries

I do believe that my testimony is great, but I have my moments. And I know I can't shy into greatness. Why do I insist on doing that? I need to get it together. The Lord is waiting on me to keep his promise. I'm holding up progress. And why? Because I don't want to make too much noise.

Myla Denise

No Excuse

I've shared with you your purpose,
told you it's guaranteed
that you'll have a fulfilling life
with inspirational prosperity
I've purposely put people in your life
to show you the various stages
of where your life will be
in hopes that their boldness would be contagious
I know that you believe in me
but I want to increase your faith
I want you to step out
with power leading the way
what is the worst that can happen
if you go after my plan for you actively
not by being passive
and calling that waiting patiently
your time is coming
but there are things you must do before
I can even give you
a small portion of what's in store
what more do you need from me
what shall I say that you haven't heard
there's not much else I can give to you
besides my promise and my word
what is your excuse for not giving
and putting in your all
do you really think I'd let you get this far
just to let you fall
who is it that you are afraid of
and can cause you to eclipse
all of your heart's desires
and your largest wish
what is causing you to be so timid
when your testimony has such strength
what is so scary to you
that keeps you from obeying
what can I do to prove to you
that I've got your best interests in mind
that I haven't already dropped
in your spirit time after time
you've already survived the worst part

Dawn: Diary of a Poet

and I need you to understand
that my next level of blessing and healing
requires you to take a more active stance
I'm pleading to you to fully trust me
by making some deliberate changes today
stop permitting your fear to be
bigger than your faith

Diary Entries

I heard Sheryl Brady preach last night and she preached! She came from Genesis. Talked about how Noah did what God told him, no questions asked. Just did it. Just because God told him to. That's what I need to do. Publish this book just because I know God told me to. No questions asked.

*****

When we pray, do we hear the answers God gives or the ones we choose to receive?

*****

The more I resist, the more I diminish what God has for me.

Dawn: Diary of a Poet

His Answer

Tired of going to friends with issues, I decided to go to the source
I looked up to God, with my hands raised and asked, what is all the
struggling for?
He asked me if I believed that he was taking me higher
Then said to me, to whom much is given, much shall be required
Told me he gives us all the choice
To follow his word or be guided by another voice
Those who hurt you chose the wrong thing
So I asked him, what does that have to do with me?
They chose, not me, so why did I have to tolerate
Effects of their decisions, why was that my fate?
You left me without a choice, feels like my entire life
Has been based on someone else's decisions, that doesn't seem right
He responded, your life, from this point on is based on what you choose
You can only be influenced now by what others do
Back then you didn't have much to decide
That was based on someone else's decisions, you are right
But I saw you then, as I still see you today
Hear all your cries, feel all your pain
I recognize that this may not put your mind at much ease
But you were chosen, hand selected by me
I knew what you were capable of and who you would become
I knew what you would be today and what you would come from
I knew that you would work this out and press your way through
I knew how you would react and which direction you would choose
I knew that this process would shape and mold your being
And that it would prepare you for all that I was bringing
I allowed all that to happen because I could see you at the end
And all along the way, I kept whispering in your spirit, 'you win'
I've made you stronger, your endurance lasts longer,
you know how to persevere
I've taught you to fight, value your life
and to trust in me despite uncertainty and fear
You understand the need for compassion through these actions
and it is in you so intensely
Your heart is so open for those who've been broken
because of what you had to endure silently
And my will all along was to make you strong
so that you could handle what I've intended you to
Your great desire to become an inspirational writer
will come to pass because I put that in you
I gave you the talent, but more importantly

Myla Denise

I've given you credibility because you had to trust in me
I've directly deposited in you the adequate words to say
Because you had to repeat them to yourself everyday
I've allowed you to understand the pain so that others will
Trust what you say because you've felt how they feel
And that desire, the most intense of all
Was given to you because you had to rise from a fall
So your heartaches and trials have become the means
To which I've been able to instill and fulfill your most desired dreams

Diary Entries

I bought and read No More Sheets by Juanita Bynum today. I loved what she said on page 27. "You are responsible to tell your story..." I know in my soul that I am to tell my story. Mainly because I do not want to. She went on to say, "If you dare to step out in faith and be transparent, I believe you will find the bridge that leads you into a more liberated life." I so needed that. I am missing my liberation and my getting involved in ministry will put me there. My freedom will come from exposing. By helping to set others free, I'll be freed. I need to be transparent.

*****

God watches over us and it is my hope that everybody who looks at me will think the same. I so want my life to be an example of what God can do if you trust him and say yes. I so want people to see my life and say if she made it then so can I. I hope I can lead other people to step out on faith because they'll see what happened to me when I did it.

*****

I realized something...just because I still have memories of being fondled doesn't mean it hurts. I still think about it, but it doesn't hurt. I have questions. Like why did all of them approach me? How do they see or think of me now? Do each of them know about what the others did? And how can I use my experiences to live a better life? I know it's not going to destroy me or my spirit so it has to help me.

*****

On the way back from Indianapolis I was thinking about [my friend] and how I wanted to tell her I'd seen [an abuser] and it made me feel strange. I wanted to tell her how odd it is to see him and how I feel guilty about what I'm about to expose. As we're on the road listening to V103 a song came on that I feel was no coincidence. It was Yolanda Adams' The Battle is the Lord's. I'm going to walk in that. The battle is not mine. I just have to do what he says. He'll take care of the outcome. The guilt is not mine either.

*****

Speak life. Think life. Dream life.

Myla Denise

The Battle

Lord, I know you were there every single time
including the instances I can't recall
holding the pieces of my heart in your hands
as my soul braced itself for a major fall
I know you were there for every offense
waiting to carry me on to the next phase
but I couldn't find words to ask for help
all I could do was mourn in your face
you gently urged me with tears in your eyes
to unlock my heart and leave it on your throne
but I was too afraid to open up
so I held a face and heart of stone
my smiled was fixed, laughter was a reflex
kindness came out, but nothing could enter
I forced myself to be sunshine,
yet my soul was a constant state of winter
you told me that I could never go beyond
what my mind tortured me with
if I never opened my heart to free myself
and trust you to heal me through your spirit
then you showed me what you had planned for my life
and told me I was my greatest barrier
and when I cried that I didn't have the strength to go on
you said you would be my carrier
when I answered with hesitancy, you asked,
"how do you think you made it all this time
who do you think has saved you
maintaining your soul and your right mind
I've kept you up to this point
but you have gone as far as you can
without freely exposing your hurts to me
and completely leaving your healing in my hands,"
the desire was there for me to be free
but I wasn't sure what else I could do
I had already looked in the mirror countless times
and gave a play-by-play of what I'd gone through
I heard that this was therapeutic,
calling the cause of my hurt by its name
but all I was doing was admitting what I already knew
I never expressed the extent of my pain
you told me to just tell you what was in my heart
not what was intellectual or academic

Dawn: Diary of a Poet

I had been trying to get healing by stating facts
and never letting my emotions in it
and once I finally let you know
that I wanted to do all that you asked
you took me back to where I'd been running from
and told me it was time to face my past
what I'd been desperately avoiding
was suddenly directly in my face
but before I could run, like I'd always done
you covered me in your love and grace
you encouraged me to continue
constantly saying that you were there with me
told me to simply trust in your process
and I would be healed permanently
so I put the work in and for months
I went through therapy with you, Lord
each time I made progress you gave me larger pieces
of the puzzle that you initially had in store
and what I told you I couldn't handle
became my heart's strongest aspiration
and all I desire to do is encourage others who
can identify with abuse and manipulation
I want to tell people to hold on
convince them that if you could heal my grief
then you can do the same for them
just like you have done for me
it has become my entire life's purpose
to share what I'd previously tried to conceal
and now I will tell the story to all who will listen
if it will lead people's hearts to be healed
Lord, I just want to thank you for being there
from the first day that this process begun
and for constantly reassuring me when I had doubts
that the battle was already won

Diary Entries

I've come to the conclusion that I'm healed of that situation. It doesn't bother me to think of those things that happened to me all those years ago. I can't even say what did it. I just understand how blessed I am regardless. I've managed in spite of and that is encouraging. Now I realize that none of it was fair or just, but it hasn't limited the quality of my life. I'm not crazy now or pregnant with a kid or depressed. I'm fine. I'm better than fine. I'm grateful. It took ten years, but it's worth it. And I still desire to help others that experienced something similar. Help them to see that as hard as it is, it's not impossible to get through to the other side. And getting to the other side is so rewarding. To know where I've come from and to be where I am now is such a joy. An internal joy that can't be removed by external situations. I'll always have this. I'll always know the strength I've been given to get where I am. That cannot be taken away.

*****

Susan L. Taylor says in Lessons in Living, Your grandest dreams are all within your reach. If it weren't so, God wouldn't have put the desire so deeply in your soul. Then on the next page she says there are no dreams too great to dream, no ambitious or goals too lofty to achieve. We have the inner vision, wisdom and strength to create the life we want, if we will. I love that.

Dawn: Diary of a Poet

In His Presence

I can sense your presence so very intensely
in the pit of my soul, I know you are moving
my life's successes are getting to a place
where they can no longer be logically explained
the people that have been in my life are no accident
their dreams intermingle with mine and it's no mere coincidence
the same ones that were a part of my life before I had an inkling
of the visions you outlined for me and are now manifesting
are the very blessings that are encouraging me to increase my dream
and the thought of how intricate this plan has been is astonishing
I can sense your presence so very intensely
and I can't believe this has been your goal from the beginning
you have guided my spirit in the seemingly small, mundane events
but still made me feel like I had a choice in all this
thank you for teaching me that when you say that something will be
there is absolutely nothing that can stop it, not even me
not inadequate qualifications, education or a short list of contacts
because with you on my side, I don't need to concern myself with any of that
not even when I try hiding a lack of faith behind low self-esteem
because my talent has little to do with my ability, it's you working in me
I can sense your presence so very intensely
in everything that I do and with all that is within me
I've stopped being a puppet to what it looks and feels like
because those are sensory perceptions and this is a spiritual life
and my emotions can keep me bound, reluctant and disobedient
preventing me to reach beyond comfort zones to get what you sent
and there are people depending on my testimony so they can be encouraged
it is an awesome responsibility that I cannot afford to play with
and while there are moments when I may think it's overwhelming
they don't outweigh how honored I am that you entrusted such to me
I can sense your presence so very intensely
I've started walking in a new level of joy and peace
recognizing that I am fully defined by your words and nothing less
whatever qualities you embody, I will work to possess
and now that my will for my life is in alignment with yours
there is nothing I cannot do and am not sufficiently equipped to work toward
I trust you completely, not my abilities or anyone else's guarantee
and now that I've fully released my life in your hands, I am totally free
free to sense your presence so very intensely
free to allow the presence of you to fill me completely

Diary Entries

It's time for me to know who I am. God's plan for my life is going to go forth with or without my cooperation. I'm not big enough to stop my own destiny and if I'm not big enough and I have God on my side then no one or nothing else can stop it either.

*****

I'm loving Vickie Yohe's song, Because of Who You Are. It is on repeat...only because I keep hitting play. I read a scripture that brought tears to my eyes. It was 1 Corinthians 7:22. For he who is called in the Lord while a slave is the Lord's freedman. That spoke to me. I was a slave to grief, sadness, denial, hurt, self pity, pretending and the past. And the Lord called me anyway. Verse 20 says, Let each one remain in the same calling in which he was called. I was called to encourage hearts. I will remain in that calling whether it's through poems, novels or public speaking. As long as I remain the Lord's freedman I am available.

Dawn: Diary of a Poet

Where Do I Go From Here?

When I asked myself what I intended to get out of sharing such a personal work, the answer had nothing to do with expressing artistic talent or lyrical skills. My desire for releasing this project was to help people. I wanted to show that whatever you are suffering with or suffered with at one time was not solely experienced by you. I wanted you to know that you are not, nor have you ever been, alone.

Some can directly identify with my exact situation, but others of you may have related to the pain expressed, but not the cause. Rest assured that hurt is hurt. Pain is pain. The source of the emotion is really not that important. How to work through that emotion is most important. Whether your story is like mine or not, I could not put out a collection with such emotion and simply leave you in your grief, anger, fear and confusion.

I highly recommend that you find an outlet. Writing was mine, but if that is not what interests you, find something that does. In this case, what you choose as your outlet does not have to be something of which you think you are an expert. To free yourself, you only need to release what you're feeling. You could sing, speak with someone you trust, draw, dance, play an instrument, or whatever you enjoy doing that will allow your heart to be free. If you do enjoy writing or think that writing will help, you can write letters, poems or just write whatever comes to your mind. Just find a positive way to release your emotion instead of trying to act as if it doesn't exist. It will not just go away, trust me.

Another outlet could be counseling. I realize that Christians are taught that once we find God we are brand new creatures, but your past can and will follow you if you don't deal with it. Don't fall into that trap of it's just a matter of making up your mind. You do have to make up your mind that you will work through it and that you will make it, but making that decision does not make you exempt from feeling. That's why counseling was created. Use it. And if you don't believe it, what do you think pastors and bishops do when they aren't preaching and teaching?

Reading proves to be very helpful as well. There are many books on everything life throws your way. Go online or to any bookstore and you'll find subject matter that pertains to your issue. Reading can be very therapeutic in that it provides information while giving readers a sense of commonality.

I am a huge advocate of prayer. Find some quiet time and simply tell the Lord what is on your heart. If anger is what you feel, say that. If hurt is in your heart, let him know. If fear plagues you, express that fear. If you are confused about what's going on in your life or even on how to pray, just say so. Secondly, after

73

you pray, allow yourself some time to sit still. Listen. It is surprising how many people talk to God and then get up and go through their day to day routine. Prayer is important, but listening is just as important as praying. Why would you get God's attention and then not listen to what he has to say? He does answer.

Dawn: Diary of a Poet

Scriptures to Stand On

The memory of the righteous is blessed. Psalm 10:7
Because my problem lied in what I remembered, I had to pray regarding my mind. I told the Lord that I did not want to remember. I asked him to just remove the memories from me. I'm glad he knows better. As painful and tormenting as the memories were, I am glad that he did not wipe them away. I know how far he's brought me and that all things are possible considering where I've been and where I'm going.

For I am convinced that neither death, nor life, neither angels nor demons, neither the present nor the future, nor any powers, neither height nor depth, nor anything else in all creation, will be able to separate us from the love of God that is in Christ Jesus our Lord. Romans 8:38 - 39
God's love cannot be separated from you. He loves you simply because you exist. This is not as a result of what you've done or haven't done. Not even life, or anything that follows, can separate you from God's love.

For I know the thoughts that I think toward you, says the Lord, thoughts of peace and not of evil, to give you a future and a hope. Then you will call upon Me and go and pray to Me, and I will listen to you. And you will seek Me and find Me, when you search for Me with all your heart. I will be found by you, says the Lord, and I will bring you back from captivity. Jeremiah 29:11-14
There was a brief time when I considered that God didn't think very much of me because of how my life was going. Reading this scripture showed me otherwise. For God to say that he knows the thoughts he has toward me says that he definitely has thoughts toward me. I exist to God. His thoughts toward me are to give me a future and a hope. Those were things I wasn't sure I had a chance to obtain. He then says that when I pray he will listen. When I seek him, I will find him. Lastly, he will bring me back from captivity. It doesn't say he will keep from being in captivity, just that he'll bring me back. I didn't feel so bad for being there because the Lord already knew I'd get there. But he was going to bring me out.

...all things work together for the good of those that love God, to those who are called according to his purpose. Romans 8:28
When I can't see the good in a situation or I can't see the big picture, this reminds me that no matter what is going on, all things will eventually work together for my good.

The Lord is not slow in keeping his promise, as some understand slowness. He is patient with you. 2 Peter 3:9
I used to think that God was too slow in granting my requests. I wanted to walk in my healing right now. I wanted to publish books right now. I simply wanted everything right now. This reminds me that anything I'm waiting for has to be because I'm not ready and forces me to ask myself, what am I doing (or not doing) that is holding up my progress?

His favor surrounds me like a shield. Psalm 20:3
God's favor is powerful. It gives you reach education, contacts and preparations are unable to. In any situation, God's favor has the final say. To know that it surrounds me as a shield has encouraged my heart and has provided me with the confidence I've needed to face any insecurity.

The blessing of the Lord makes one rich, and he adds no sorrow with it. Proverbs 10:22
I used to think that if I exposed my life I would be doing a good thing, but there would be an excessive price to pay. I told myself I was willing to pay that price because God told me to tell my story. It wasn't until I really began to focus on this scripture that I understood that if God was directing me to tell this story for his purpose in my life, whatever followed would be good for me. That is not to say that everyone would be supportive or that everything would be perfect, but in the end I know that God is doing the increasing and there will be nothing sorrowful added to it.

What has happened to me has served to advance the gospel. Philippians 1:12
Many people find themselves asking, "Why me?" When we lose a loved one, fall ill or get mistreated we always want to know why it had to happen to us. Before I could even ask that question, I was given this answer. What is so great about this is it does not say all the suffering I endured has served to advance the gospel. It says what has happened to me, it is not limited to pain. What that suggests is everything in your life has served to advance the gospel. We want reasons why bad things happen to us, but we never ask God, "Why me," when we are blessed. Our blessings, successes and joys will also serve to advance the gospel. This encouraged me because I know that those blessings, successes and joys are on their way.

Do not fear, for I am with you, do not be dismayed, for I am your God I will strengthen you and help you; I will uphold you. Isaiah 41:10
Finding the courage to admit to those closest to me what I experienced came from focusing on this scripture. I did not think I was capable of carrying out God's instruction for my life. I thought that it was impossible and that the

consequences would be too great. Reading the words, I will uphold you, let me know 1) it isn't uncommon for me to think that I needed upholding, otherwise it wouldn't have been written and 2) that when I feel like I can't carry myself, God will carry me.

Become complete. Be of good comfort, be of one mind, live in peace; and the God of love and peace will be with you. 2 Corinthians 13:11
I love this scripture because it is very direct about what it takes to have peace and peace was what I'd been searching for most of my life. In order to have the God of love and peace with me all I have to do is make a lifetime goal of becoming complete, being of good comfort for others, as well as myself, being of one mind and living in peace. All of these instructions are aspirations that I have in my own life. The consequence for seeking out the life I already desire is the love and peace of God.

To whom much is given, much is required. Luke 12:48
More than any other scripture I have found myself repeating this one to myself over the years. The Lord has blessed me with much. I have large dreams, great visions and grand plans for my life and I realize that he is only bringing those into fruition by way of what he has required me to overcome. The more heartbreaking your experience, the more potential there is to illustrate the power of the Lord. If your life has been tainted by negativity you have the ability to be an example to others and for that you have been given much, not in terms of what you'll have to endure, but in terms of the greatness God wants to put in your life.

OTHER BOOKS BY COLE PUBLISHING

SCARS
{One Child's Painful Cry for Love} $19.⁹⁵

Becoming One Flesh (A Journey From Singlehood to Marriage)
{For the Young & Young At Heart} $15.⁰⁰

Lamentations of A Child
{Poetic Expression from Abused Children} $12.⁰⁰

Lamentations of A Man
{Poetic Expression of Conflicts} $12.⁰⁰

Lamentations of A Woman
{Poetic Expression of Inner Struggles} $12.⁰⁰

UPCOMING RELEASES

My Press Towards God
{A Journey To The Prophetic}

Name:	Date: / /	
Address:		
City:	State:	Zip Code:
Day Telephone:	Evening Telephone:	
Name of Book(s):		
Subtotal:	$.⁰⁰	
Sales Tax (CA add 8.25%):	$.⁰⁰	
Shipping & Handling (add $4.55 per book):	$.⁰⁰	
Total Due:	$.⁰⁰	

◇ Check ◇ Money Order ◇ VISA ◇ Master Charge

Credit Card No.:	Expiration Date: /
Driver's License No.:	
Signature:	Date:

MAKE CHECKS *-or-* MONEY ORDERS PAYABLE TO:
Cole Publishing
13428 Maxella Avenue, #701
Marina Del Rey, CA 90292
(310) 330-9937
Visit our Website www.candacecole.com
Feel free to contact Myla Denise at myladenise@hotmail.com